First published in Great Britain in 1996 by Brockhampton Press, a member of the Hodder Headline Group, 20 Bloomsbury Street, London WC1B 3QA.

This series of little gift books was made by Frances Banfield, Kate Brown, Laurel Clark, Penny Clarke, Clive Collins, Melanie Cumming, Nick Diggory, Deborah Gill, David Goodman, Douglas Hall, Maureen Hill, Nick Hutchison, John Hybert, Kate Hybert, Douglas Ingram, Simon London, Patrick McCreeth, Morse Modaberi, Tara Neill, Anne Newman, Grant Oliver, Michelle Rogers, Nigel Soper, Karen Sullivan and Nick Wells.

ISBN 1 86019 436 2

A copy of the CIP data is available from the British Library upon request.

Produced for Brockhampton Press by Flame Tree Publishing, a part of The Foundry Creative Media Company Limited, The Long House, Antrobus Road, Chiswick W4 5HY.

Printed and bound in Italy by L.E.G.O. Spa.

THE LITTLE BOOK

OF

Cats

Selected by Beth Hurley

'Please would you tell me,'
said Alice a little timidly ...
'why your cat grins like that?'
'It's a Cheshire cat,' said the Duchess,
'and that's why.'...
The Cat only grinned when it saw Alice.
It looked good-natured, she thought:
still it had *very* long claws and a great many teeth,
so she felt that it ought to be treated with respect.

Lewis Carroll, *Alice's Adventures in Wonderland*

When I get a cat I'm going to love it very much.

Tom, 4

To the uninitiated – especially to the true-blue
Londoner – all orange cats are 'ginger'. I have heard
them referred to as yellow cats and sandy cats and
marmalade cats by superior persons, but the voice of
the people proclaims them ginger.

Michael Joseph, *Cat's Company*

Two or three Cats
And two or three mice
Two or three sprats
At a very great price –
Two or three sandies
And two or three tabbies
Two or three dandies –
And two Mrs – mum!

John Keats, *Two or three*

There is now at the Cattery in the Devil's Point a cat
which is an expert catcher of fish, being in the constant
habit of diving into the sea and bringing up the fish
alive in her mouth, and depositing them in
the guard-room for the use of the sailors.

Plymouth Journal, 1827

God made the cat to give mankind the pleasure of
caressing the tiger.

Fernand Mery, *Her Majesty the Cat*

A. Auguste Talbo

Hey diddle diddle
The cat and the fiddle
The cow jumped over the moon;
The little dog laughed to see such sport,
And the dish ran away with the spoon.

Nursery rhyme

The most domestic cat, which has lain on a rug
all her days, appears quite at home in the woods,
and, by her sly and stealthy behaviour,
proves herself more native there
than the regular inhabitants.

Henry David Thoreau, *Walden*

... the friendliest thing,
The most stand-offish thing,
Cruellest, kindest, most loveable thing,
Softest, sweetest, most incomprehensible thing.

William Kean Seymour

How well I can understand Mohammed who, in
response to the chant of the muezzin summoning him
to prayers, cut off with a pair of scissors the hem of his
cloak before rising to his feet, for fear of disturbing his
cat, which had settled down thereon to sleep.

Pierre Loti

I am the cat of cats.
I am the everlasting cat!
Cunning and old, and sleek as jam.

W. B. Rands, 'The Cat of Cats'

Cats are a mysterious kind of folk. There is more
passing in their minds than we are aware of.

Sir Walter Scott

The cat with his phosphoric eyes,
which serve him as lanterns,
and sparks flying from his back,
fearlessly haunts the darkness, where he encounters
wandering phantoms, sorcerers, alchemists,
necromancers, resurrectionists, lovers,
pickpockets, assassins, drunken patrols,
and all those obscene larvae which sally forth
and do their work only at night.

Théophile Gautier

When I play with my cat, who knows whether she
amuses herself with me, or I with her?

Michel de Montaigne

CAT: A domestick animal that catches mice,
commonly reckoned by naturalists the lowest order
of the leonine species.

Samuel Johnson, *A Dictionary of the English Language*

Mark Twain invented ingenious names for his cats,
whom he adored.
Four kittens were called Sour Mash, Apollinaris,
Zoroaster, and Blatherskite.
Another pair were Sackcloth and Ashes.

A cat in gloves catches no mice.

Proverb

Cat! who hast pass'd thy grand climacteric,
How many mice and rats has in thy days
Destroy'd? — How many titbits stolen? Gaze
With those bright languid segments green, and prick
Those velvet ears — but pr'ythee do not stick
Thy great talons in me — and upraise
Thy gentle mew — and tell me all thy frays
Of fish and mice, and rats and tender chick.
Nay, look not down, nor lick thy dainty wrists —
For all the wheezy asthma, — and for all
Thy tail's tip is nick'd off — and though the fists
Of many a maid have given thee many a maul,
Still is that fur as soft as when the lists
In youth thou ener'dst on glass-bottled wall.

John Keats

One of the most striking differences between a cat and
a lie is that a cat has only nine lives.

Mark Twain

My dear daughter – Sorry I am to inform you of the illness of his Serene Highness the Archduke Rumpelstilzchen, Marquis Macbum, Earl Tomlemagne, Baron Raticide, Waouhler, and Skratsch. His Serene Highness is afflicted with the mange.

Letter from Robert Southey to his daughter, 31 January 1825

He scorned the inarticulate mouthings of the lower
animals. The vulgar mewing and howling of the cat
species was beneath him; he sometimes uttered a sort of
well-bred and articulate ejaculation, when he wished to
call attention to something that he considered
remarkable, or to some want of his,
but he never went whining about.

Charles Dudley Warner

The cat would eat fish, but would not wet her feet.

Proverb

As I was going to St Ives,
I met a man with seven wives;
Each wife had seven sacks,
Each sack had seven cats,
Each cat had seven kits:
Kits, cats, sacks, wives,
How many were going to St Ives?

Nursery rhyme

The Cat will kill mice, and he will be kind to babies when he is in the house, just so long as they do not pull his tail too hard. But when he has done that, and between times, and when the moon gets up and night comes, he is the Cat that walks by himself, and all places are alike to him. Then he goes out to the Wet Wild Woods or up on the Wet Wild Trees or on the Wet Wild Roofs, waving his wild tail and walking by his wild lone.

Rudyard Kipling, *The Cat Who Walked by Himself*

The pub name 'Cat and Kittens' alludes to the large and small pewter pots in which beer was served.

Ding dong bell
Pussy's in the well.
Who put her in?
Little Johnny Green.

Nursery rhyme

My cat sits on my face.

Lucy, 4

When I observed he was a fine cat, saying,
'Why yes, Sir, but I have had cats whom I liked
better than this'; and then, as if
perceiving Hodge to be out of countenance,
adding, 'but he is a very fine cat,
a very fine cat indeed.'

Boswell, *Life of Johnson*

Pussy cat, pussy cat, where have you been?
I've been up to London to visit the queen.
Pussy cat, pussy cat, what did you there?
I frightened a little mouse under her chair.

Nursery rhyme

Careful observers may foretell the hour
(By sure prognostics) when to dread a shower;
While rain depends, the pensive cat gives o'er
Her frolics, and pursues her tail no more.

Jonathan Swift

There are no ordinary cats.

Colette

The cat is mighty dignified until the dog comes by.

Folk saying

The smallest feline is a masterpiece.

Leonardo da Vinci

The forepaws of Siamese cats 'are gloved almost to the shoulder like the long black kid arms of Yvette Guilbert'.

Aldous Huxley

Since each of us is blessed with only one life, why not live it with a cat?

Robert Stearns

Curiosity killed the cat. Satisfaction brought it back.

Proverb

THIS is the very nicest cat
  That ever learnt to purr.
Her eyes are green, but what of that?
  She has most lovely fur.

She's very useful too,
      you know;
  She keeps away
      the mice.
I love my dear
  old pussy so—
  Now, don't
  you think
    she's
    nice?

Even overweight cats instinctively know the cardinal
rule: when fat, arrange yourself in slim poses.

John Weitz

A white cat was staring at some goldfish,
she sat very, very still,
but now and then the tip of her tail twitched
as if it were alive.
Peter thought it best to go away
without speaking to her;
he had heard about cats from his cousin,
little Benjamin Bunny.

Beatrix Potter, *The Tale of Peter Rabbit*

Hey, my kitten, my kitten,
And hey my kitten, my deary!
Such a sweet pet as this
There is not far nor neary.
Here we go up, up, up,
Here we go down, down, downy;
Here we go backwards and forwards,
And here we go round, round, roundy.

Jonathan Swift, *The Nurse's Song*

Now cat's done
mewing, bedroom's
touched by moonlight.

Basho, Haiku

If a fish is the movement of water embodied, given
shape, then a cat is a diagram and pattern of subtle air.

Doris Lessing

Honest as the cat when the meat is out of reach.

English proverb

There was a crooked man,
and he walked a crooked mile,
He found a crooked sixpence against a crooked stile:
He bought a crooked cat,
which caught a crooked mouse,
And they all lived together
in a little crooked house.

Traditional saying

Who's that ringing at my door bell?
I'm a little pussy-cat and I'm not very well.
Then rub your little nose with a little mutton fat,
And that's the best thing for a sick pussy cat.

D'Arcy Wentworth Thompson, *That Little Black Cat*

It doesn't do to be sentimental about cats;
the best ones don't respect you for it.

Susan Howatch

Cats are smarter than men ... they never question how
much money you spend on phone calls.

Beverly Guhl

Some cats, as we all know, are born in full evening
dress. White shirt, white tie ... black tails and all. I love
cats in evening dress; they wear it so much more
elegantly than we do.

Beverley Nichols, *Cats' A-Z*

Pussy cat Mole jumped over a coal
And in her best petticoat burnt a great hole.
Poor pussy's weeping, she'll have no more milk
Until her best petticoat's mended with silk.

Pussy Cat Miaow

Stately, kindly, lordly friend,
Condescend
Here to sit by me, and turn
Glorious eyes that smile and burn,
Golden eyes, love's lustrous meed,
On the golden page I read.

Algernon Swinburne, *To a Cat*

Mrs Crupp had indignantly assured him that there wasn't room to swing a cat there; but, as Mr Dick justly observed to me, sitting down on the foot of the bed, nursing his leg, 'You know, Trotwood, I don't want to swing a cat. I never do swing a cat. Therefore, what does that signify to *me*?'

Charles Dickens, *David Copperfield*

I don't know whether I would like a cat because it might scratch my rabbit.

Hannah, 4

I have a cat and he has diabetes but I love him.

Andrew, 6

'All right,' said the Cat; and this time it vanished quite slowly, beginning with the end of the tail, and ending with the grin, which remained some time after the rest of it had gone. 'Well! I've often seen a cat without a grin,' thought Alice, 'but a grin without a cat! It's the most curious thing I ever saw in all my life!'

Lewis Carroll, *Alice's Adventures in Wonderland*

Dame Trot and her cat
Sat down for a chat.
The Dame sat on this side
The cat sat on that.
Puss says the Dame
Can you catch a rat
Or a mouse in the dark?
Purr says the cat.

Anonymous

I love little pussy,
Her coat is so warm,
And if I don't hurt her
She'll do me no harm.
So I'll not pull her tail,
Nor drive her away,
But pussy and I
Very gently will play.
She shall sit by my side,
And I'll give her some food;
And pussy will love me,
Because I am good.

Jane Taylor

Tim ... exuded a remarkable benignity,
clearly the fruits of a settled wisdom that had tested the
world, with all its other creatures, and decided that it
was worth making the best of.

Bernard Levin, *Enthusiasms*

There are two means of refuge from
the miseries of life: music and cats.

Albert Schweitzer

A dog will flatter you but you have to flatter a cat.
A dog is an employee; the cat is a free-lance.

George Mikes, *How To Be a Brit*

Pussicat, wussicat, with a white foot,
When is your wedding, and I'll come to it.
The beer's to brew, the bread's to bake,
Pussy cat, pussy cat, don't be too late!

Traditional rhyme

Cats will let us love them, in fact they plainly wish us
to, but they will not love us in return, though many of
us delude ourselves that they do. On the other hand ...
they do not pretend to reciprocate our feelings, they
make no promises that they cannot or will not keep,
and they swear no empty vows.

Bernard Levin, *Enthusiasms*

Here lies the dear old station cat.
She killed some mice and many a rat.
Her days are gone, she did her best.
And now in peace she's laid to rest.

Epitaph on a cat's grave at Goodwick Railway Station

Pussy cat sits beside the fire,
So pretty and so fair.
In walks the little dog,
Ah, Pussy, are you there?
How do you do, Mistress Pussy?
I thank you kindly, little dog,
I'm very well just now.

Song for the nursery

Old Mr Bunny had no opinion whatever of cats.

Beatrix Potter, *The Tale of Benjamin Bunny*

If a man could be crossed with a cat, it would
improve man but it would deteriorate the cat.

Mark Twain

There's no need for a piece of sculpture in a home
that has a cat.

Wesley Bates

I saw a girl just like a cat
I saw a kitten wear a hat
I saw a man who saw these too,
And says, though strange,
they all are true.

Anonymous

The greater cats with golden eyes
Stare out between the bars.
Deserts are there, and different skies,
And night with different stars.

Vita Sackville-West, *The Greater Cats*

I have come to respect cats even more than I did.
...What graceful, complicated, infuriating, delightful
animals they are, and what a privilege to be able to
share a room, or a life, with one of them.

Desmond Morris, *Catlore*

There were two cats of Kilkenny
Each thought there was one cat too many;
So they fought and they fit,
Till, excepting their nails
And the tips of their tails
Instead of two cats, there weren't any.

Anonymous, *The Cats of Kilkenny*

Sole guardians of a nation's cheese!

John Gay

I have noticed that what cats most appreciate
in a human being is not the ability to produce food
which they take for granted –
but his or her entertainment value.

Geoffrey Household, *Rogue Male*

In the United States the figure for cat food sales
exceeds that for baby food.

Desmond Morris, *Catlore*

Are cats lazy?
Well more power to them if they are.
Which one of us has not entertained the dream of
doing just as he likes, when and how he likes, and as
much as he likes?

Fernand Mery, *Her Majesty the Cat*

'Not like cats?'
cried the Mouse in a shrill, passionate voice.
'Would you like cats if you were me?'
Lewis Carroll, *Alice's Adventures in Wonderland*

Cats seem to go on the principle that
it never does any harm to ask for what you want.
Joseph Wood Krutch, *Twelve Seasons*

Butter's movements were always cautious in the
extreme. She tiptoed about as though walking on
thin ice, hesitating at corners and peering suspiciously
round doorways until we were almost as nervous
as she was. It was the Mafia we gathered.
Joyce Fussey, *Cats in the Coffee*

The cat does not negotiate with the mouse.
Robert K. Massie

I like cats because they are yummy.

Louise, 7

When the tea is brought at five o'clock,
And all the neat curtains are drawn with care,
The little black cat with bright green eyes
Is suddenly purring there.

Harold Monro, *Milk for the Cat*

The night is a big black cat
The moon is her topaz eye,

G. Orr Clark

My cat likes being stroked behind his ear.

Matthew, 4

NOTES ON ILLUSTRATIONS

Page 5 *Four Kittens*, by C. Wilson (Cavin Graham Gallery, London). Courtesy of The Bridgeman Art Library; **Page 8-9** *Cats with a Chess Board*, by Agnes Augusta Talboys (City of Bristol Museum & Art Gallery). Courtesy of The Bridgeman Art Library; **Page 11** *The Cat in Whittington Gardens*, by Nigella Bittleson (Guildhall Art Gallery, Corporation of London). Courtesy of The Bridgeman Art Library; **Page 12-13** *A Frolic*, by Charles Edward Wilson (Bonhams, London). Courtesy of The Bridgeman Art Library; **Page 14** *Wisteria Cat*, by Ditz (Private Collection). Courtesy of The Bridgeman Art Library; **Page 16-17** *A Good Game*, by Frederick French (Bonhams, London). Courtesy of The Bridgeman Art Library; **Page 18** *Who's the Fairest of Them All?*, by Frank Paton (Bonhams, London). Courtesy of The Bridgeman Art Library; **Page 20** *Cat-Spread*, by Ditz (Private Collection). Courtesy of The Bridgeman Art Library; **Page 23** Detail from *Cats with a Chess Board*, by Agnes Augusta Talboys (City of Bristol Museum & Art Gallery). Courtesy of The Bridgeman Art Library; **Page 24-5** *Kittens at Play*, by Leon-Charles Huber (Christie's, London). Courtesy of The Bridgeman Art Library; **Page 26** *Collection du Chat Noir*, by Steinlen (Private Collection). Courtesy of The Bridgeman Art Library; **Page 29** *Milk for the Kitten*, by Johan Caspar Herterich (Christie's, London). Courtesy of The Bridgeman Art Library; **Page 30** *The Tight-Rope Dancer*. Courtesy of The Laurel Clark Collection; **Page 33** *This Is the Very Nicest Cat, That Ever Learnt to Purr*. Courtesy of The Laurel Clark Collection; **Page 34-5** *The Mischief Makers*, by Bessie Bamber (Chadwick Gallery, Warwickshire). Courtesy of The Bridgeman Art Library; **Page 36-7** *A Class Outing*, by Louis Wain (Bonhams, London). Courtesy of The Bridgeman Art Library; **Page 38** *Feeding the Kitten*, by C. H. Blair (Bonhams, London). Courtesy of The Bridgeman Art Library; **Page 40** *The Mischief Makers*, by Bessie Bamber (Chadwick Gallery, Warwickshire). Courtesy of The Bridgeman Art Library; **Page 42** *The Land of Fun*. Courtesy of The Laurel Clark. **Page 45** *Cat with a Basket*, by Charles Van Den Eycken (Cavin Graham Gallery, London). Courtesy of The Bridgeman Art Library; **Page 46** *Crotchets & Quavers*. Courtesy of The Laurel Clark Collection; **Page 48-9** *Off to Jericho*. Courtesy of The Laurel Clark Collection; **Page 51** *Don't Forget Us*. Courtesy of The Laurel Clark Collection; **Page 52** *This Is the Very Nicest Cat, That Ever Learnt to Purr*. Courtesy of The Laurel Clark Collection; **Page 55** *Punch & Judy*, by Derold Page (Private Collection). Courtesy of The Bridgeman Art Library; **Page 25** *Four Kittens*, by C. Wilson (Cavin Graham Gallery, London). Courtesy of The Bridgeman Art Library.

Acknowledgements: The Publishers wish to thank everyone who gave permission to reproduce the quotes in this book. Every effort has been made to contact the copyright holders, but in the event that an oversight has occurred, the publishers would be delighted to rectify any omissions in future editions of this book. Children's quotes printed courtesy of Herne Hill School; *The Cat Who Walked by Himself*, Rudyard Kipling, reprinted courtesy of Macmillan Publishers; *Cats and More Cats*, Doris Lessing reprinted courtesy of Michael Joseph, copyright Doris Lessing Productions Ltd, 1967, 1989; extracts from *Cats' A–Z* © Beverley Nichols, 1977; *The Tale of Peter Rabbit*, Beatrix Potter, reprinted courtesy of Frederick Warne, a division of Penguin Books; *The Tale of Benjamin Bunny*, Beatrix Potter, reprinted courtesy of Frederick Warne, a division of Penguin Books; *Enthusiasms*, Bernard Levin, reprinted courtesy of Jonathan Cape, a division of Random House UK; *Cat's Company*, Michael Joseph, reprinted courtesy of Michael Joseph, a division of Reed Books.